BEGINNING PIANO SOLO

TOP HITS

of 2016

ISBN 978-1-4950-7340-3

HAL•LEONARD®

7777 W. BLUEMOUND RD. P.O. BOX 13819 MILWAUKEE, WI 53213

Visit Hal Leonard Online at
www.halleonard.com

CONTENTS

CAN'T STOP THE FEELING

from TROLLS

Words and Music by JUSTIN TIMBERLAKE,
MAX MARTIN and SHELLBACK

Moderate Funk groove

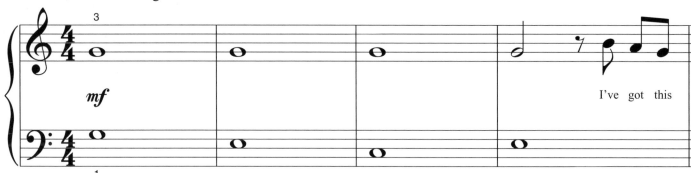

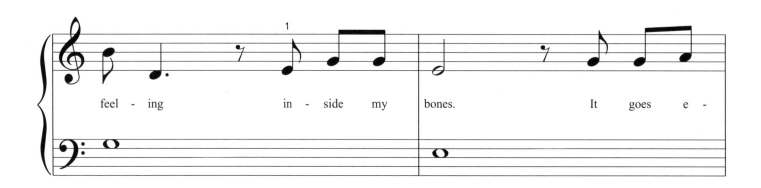

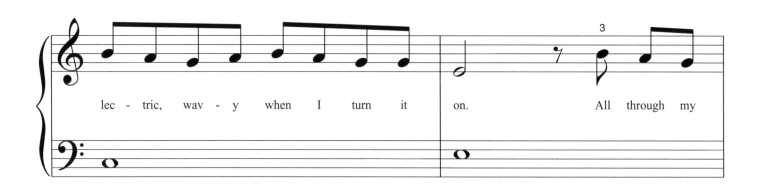

up, no ceil - ing, when we in our zone. I got that

sun - shine in my pock - et, got that good soul in my feet. I feel that

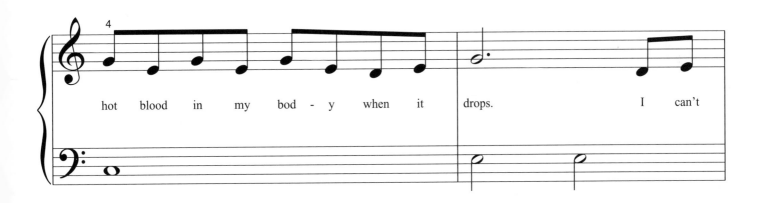

hot blood in my bod - y when it drops. I can't

take my eyes up off it, mov - ing so phe - nom - e - nal - ly. Room on

lock the way we rock it, so don't stop. Un - der the

lights when ev - 'ry - thing goes, _____ no - where to hide when I'm get - ting you

close. _____ When we move, well, you al - read - y

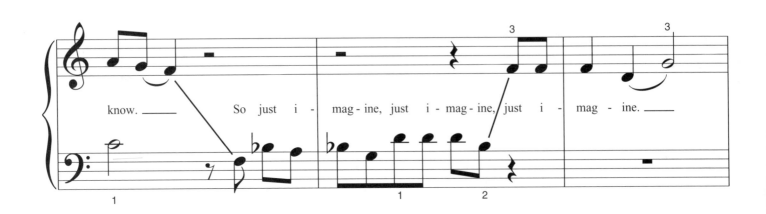

know. ____ So just i - mag - ine, just i - mag - ine, just i - mag - ine. ____

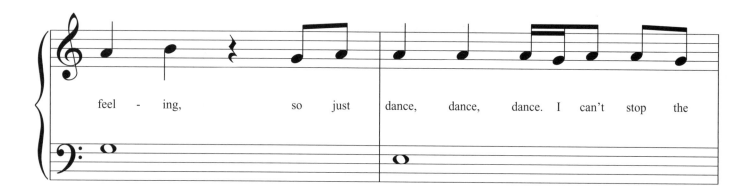

feel - ing,   so just   dance,   dance,   dance. I can't stop the

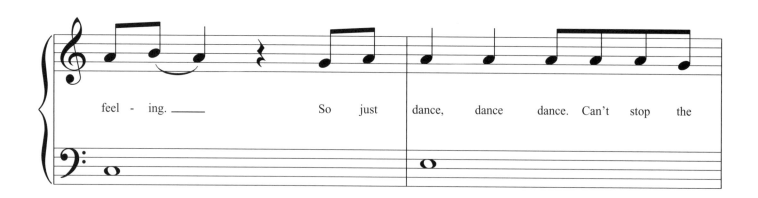

feel - ing. _____   So just   dance,   dance   dance. Can't stop the

feel - ing.   So just   dance,   dance,   dance. Can't stop the

feel - ing. _____   So keep   danc - ing.   Mm. _____

JUST LIKE FIRE

from ALICE THROUGH THE LOOKING GLASS (WDP)

Words and Music by ALECIA MOORE,
MAX MARTIN, SHELLBACK
and OSCAR HOLTER

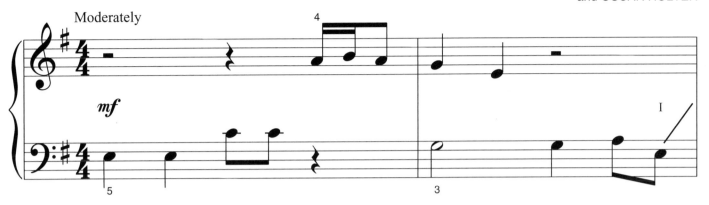

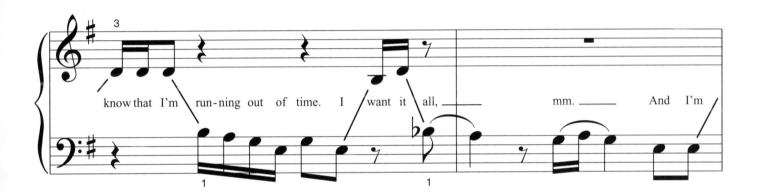

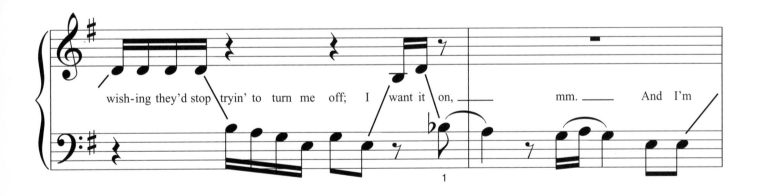

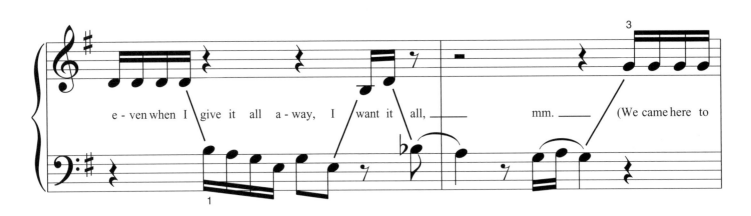

e - ven when I give it all a - way, I want it all, ____ mm. ____ (We came here to

run it, run it, run it. We came here to run it, run it,

run it.) Just like fi - re, burn-ing up the way, if I can light the

world up for just one day, watch this mad - ness, col - or - ful cha - rade. No one can

be just like me an-y-way. Just like mag-ic, I'll be fly-ing free. I'm-a dis-ap-

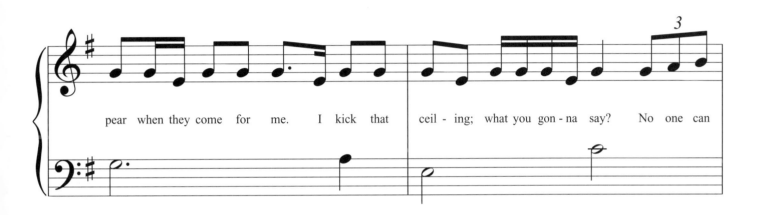

pear when they come for me. I kick that ceil-ing; what you gon-na say? No one can

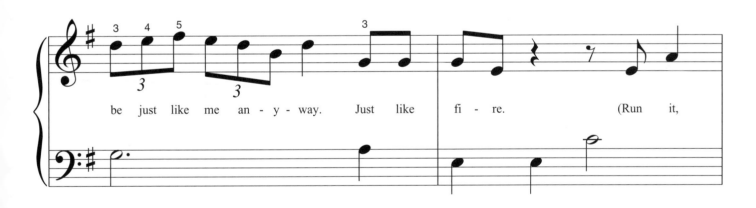

be just like me an-y-way. Just like fi-re. (Run it,

run it. We came here to run it, run it, run it.)

HOLD BACK THE RIVER

Words and Music by JAMES BAY
and IAIN ARCHER

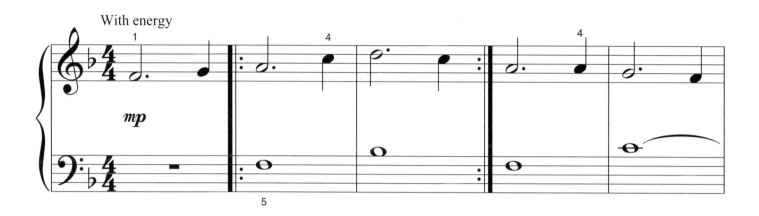

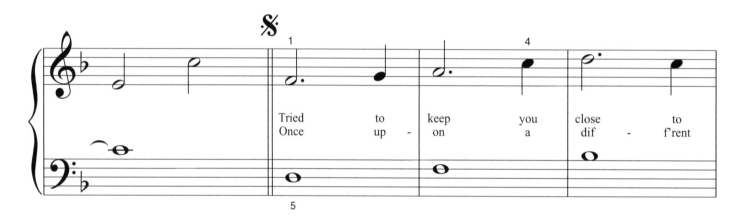

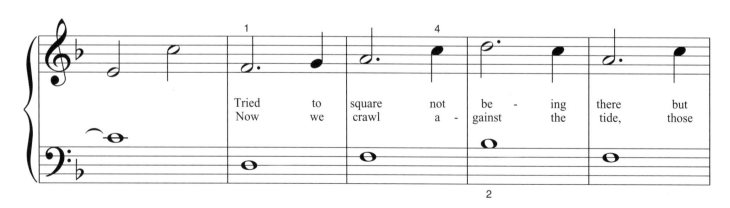

To Coda

think   that   I   should have been.
dis - tant   days   are   flash - ing   by.

Hold   back   the   riv - er,   let   me   look   in   your   eyes.   Hold   back   the   riv - er   so

I _____ can   stop   for   a   min - ute   and   see   where   you   hide.

D.S. al Coda

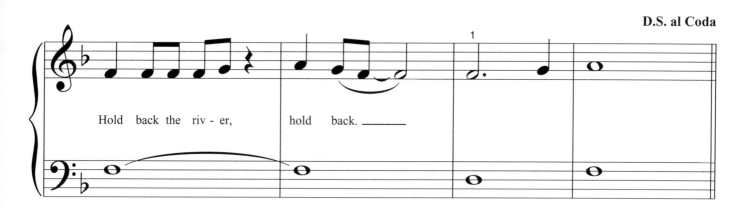

Hold   back   the   riv - er,   hold   back. _____

14

CODA

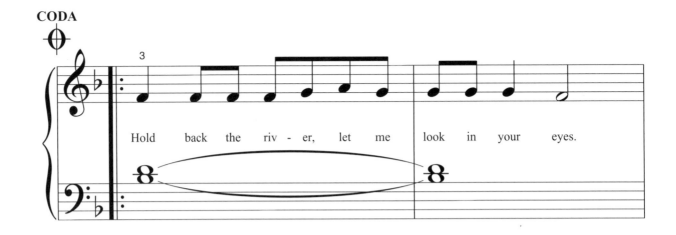

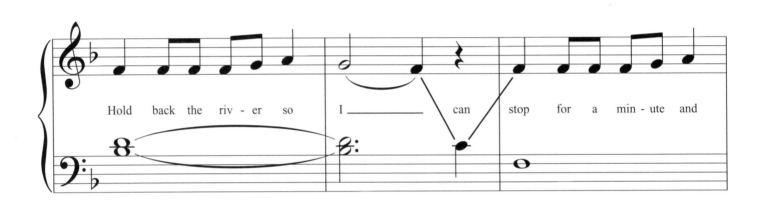

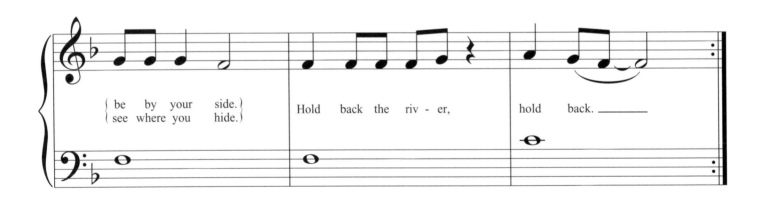

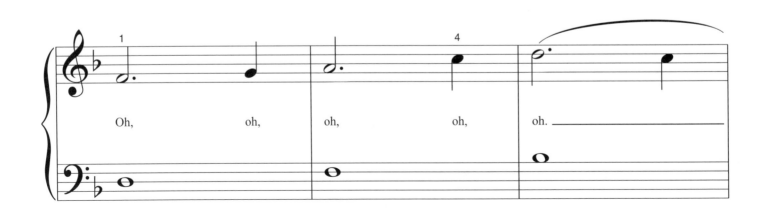

Oh, oh, ____ oh. ____

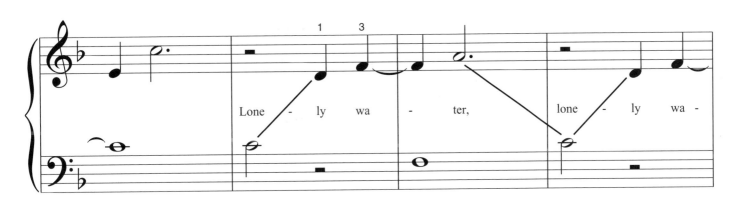

Lone - ly wa - ter, lone - ly wa -

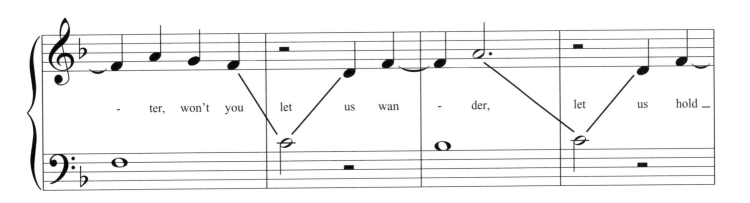

- ter, won't you let us wan - der, let us hold ___

___ each oth - er? Lone - ly wa - ter, lone - ly wa -

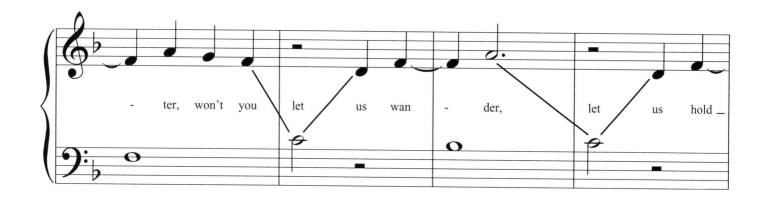

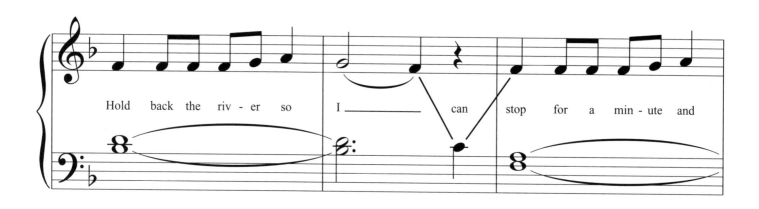

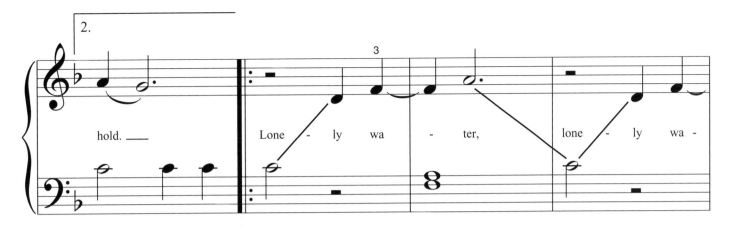

hold. ____   Lone - ly wa - ter,   lone - ly wa -

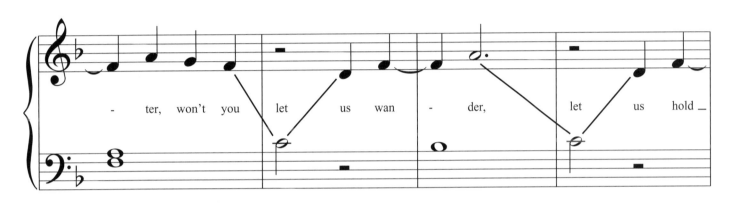

- ter, won't you let us wan - der,   let us hold ___

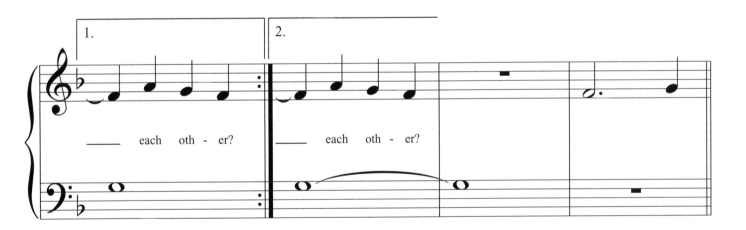

____ each oth - er?   ____ each oth - er?

H.O.L.Y.

Words and Music by busbee,
NATE CYPHERT and WILLIAM WIIK LARSEN

Moderately slow

When the sun had left __ and the win-ter came __

and the sky - fall __ could on - ly bring the rain, __ I sat in dark - ness,

all bro-ken-heart-ed. I could-n't find a day __ I did-n't feel a - lone. __

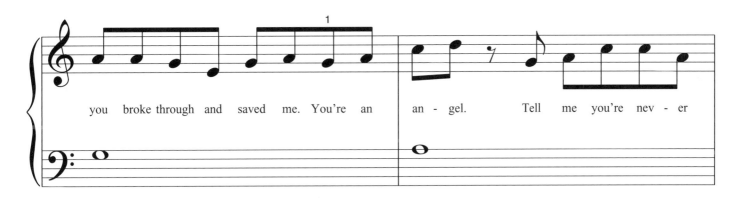

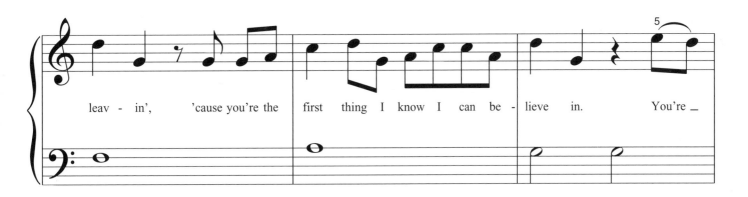

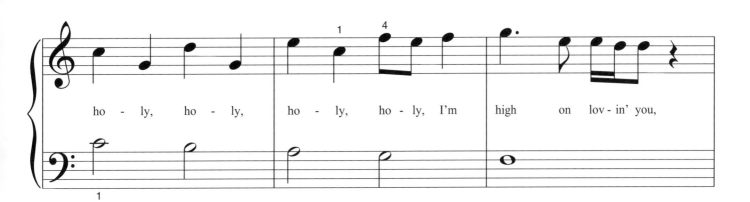

high on lov-in' you. You're _ ho - ly, ho - ly, ho - ly, ho - ly, I'm

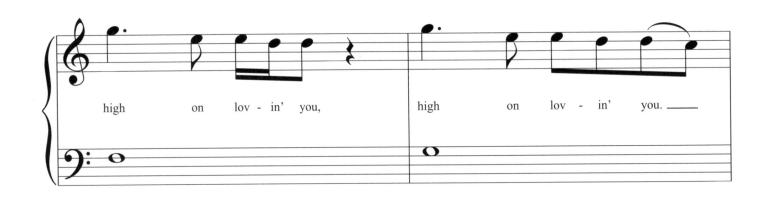

high on lov - in' you, high on lov - in' you. _

I don't need the stars, 'cause you shine for me.

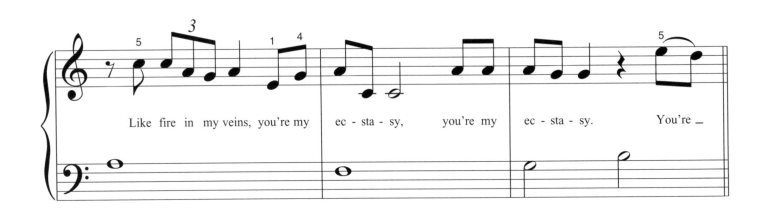

Like fire in my veins, you're my ec - sta - sy, you're my ec - sta - sy. You're _

ho - ly, ho - ly, ho - ly, ho - ly, I'm high on lov - in' you,

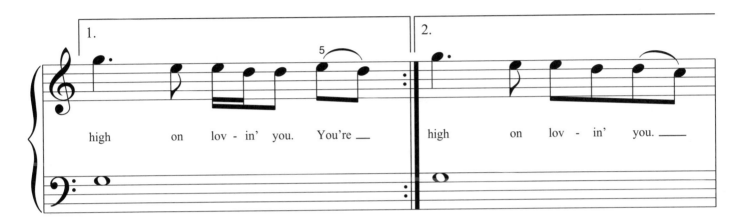

1.
high on lov - in' you. You're ___

2.
high on lov - in' you. ___

You're the heal-in' hands ___ where it used to hurt. ___ You're my sav-in' grace, ___ you're my kind of church. ___

You're ___ ho - ly. ___

LOST BOY

Words and Music by
RUTH BERHE

He came to me with the sweet - est smile; told me he want - ed to

talk for a while. He said, "Pe - ter Pan, that's what they call me.

I prom - ise that you'll nev - er be lone - ly." And ev - er

since that _____ day...

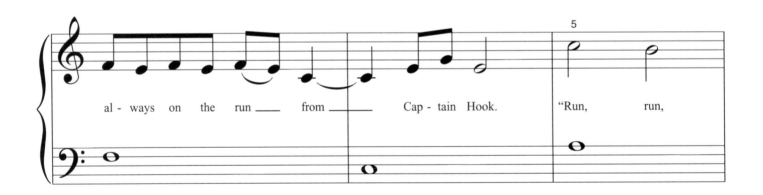

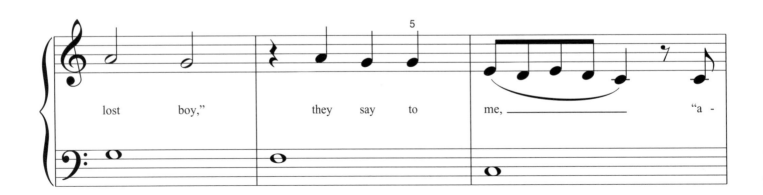

ONE CALL AWAY

Words and Music by CHARLIE PUTH,
BREYAN ISAAC, MATT PRIME,
JUSTIN FRANKS, BLAKE ANTHONY CARTER
and MAUREEN McDONALD

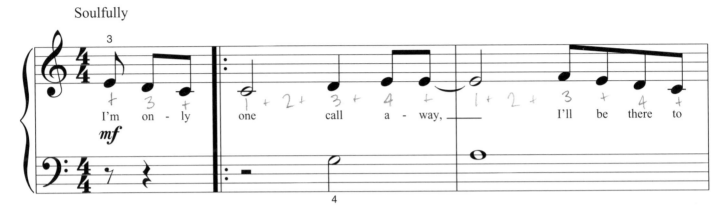

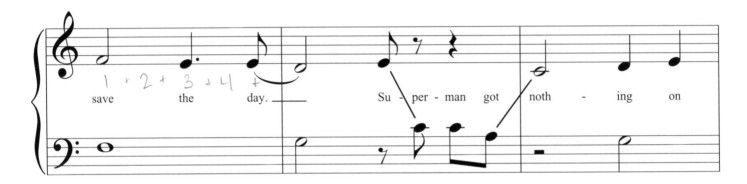

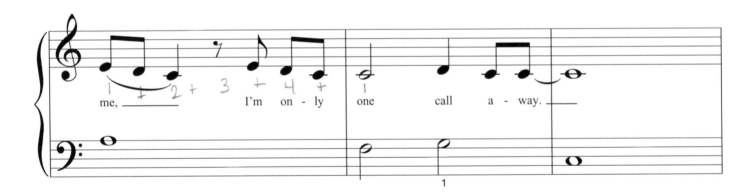

love.
free.

take a chance. No
an - y - where. For

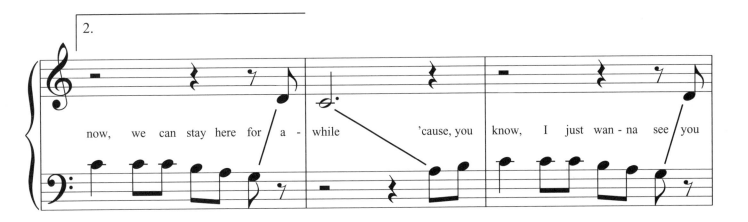
now, we can stay here for a - while

smile. _____ No

one call a - way, _____ I'll be there to save the day. _____

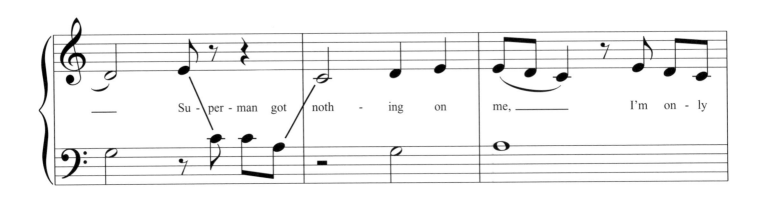

_____ Su - per - man got noth - ing on me, _____ I'm on - ly

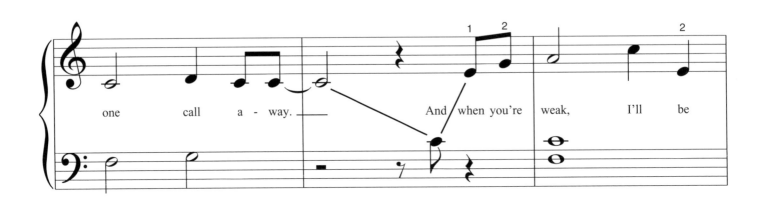

one call a - way. _____ And when you're weak, I'll be

strong. I'm gon - na keep hold - ing on. Now, don't you

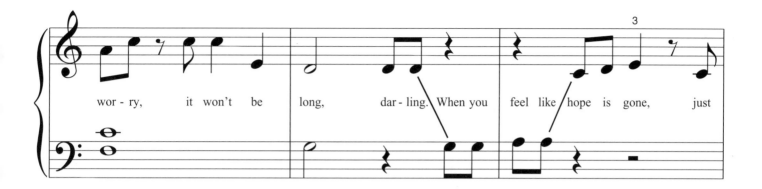

wor - ry, it won't be long, dar - ling. When you feel like hope is gone, just

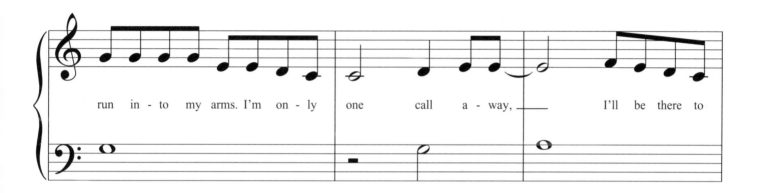

run in - to my arms. I'm on - ly one call a - way, I'll be there to

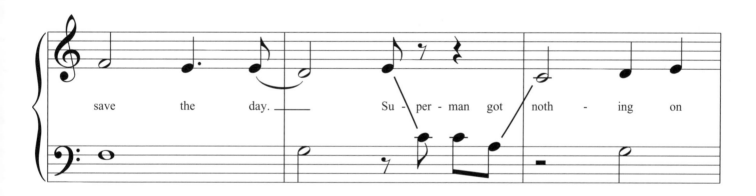

save the day. Su - per - man got noth - ing on

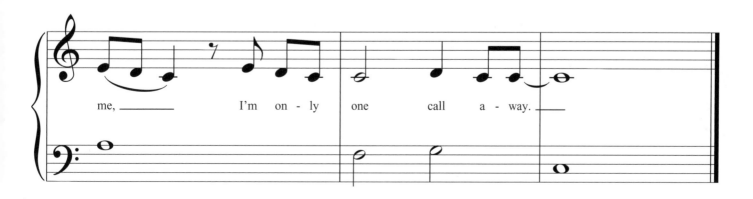

me, I'm on - ly one call a - way.

TRAVELLER

Words and Music by
CHRIS STAPLETON

Moderate two-beat

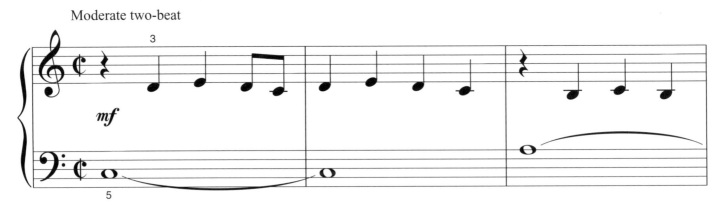

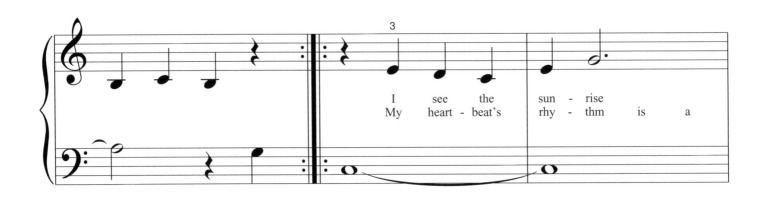

I see the sun - rise
My heart - beat's rhy - thm is a

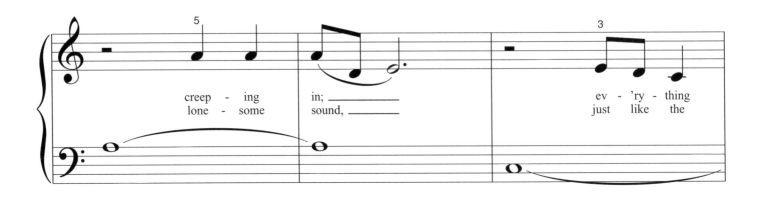

creep - ing in; _____
lone - some sound, _____

ev - 'ry - thing
just like the

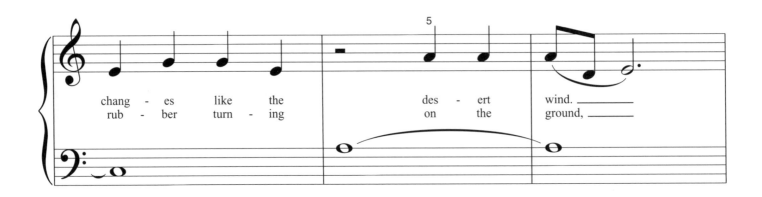

chang - es like the
rub - ber turn - ing

des - ert
on the

wind. _____
ground, _____

Here she comes, and then she's gone a-
al - ways lost _____ and _____ no - where

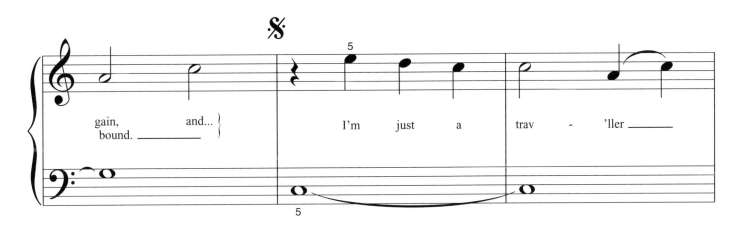

gain, and...
bound. _____
I'm just a trav - 'ller _____

on this earth, sure as my

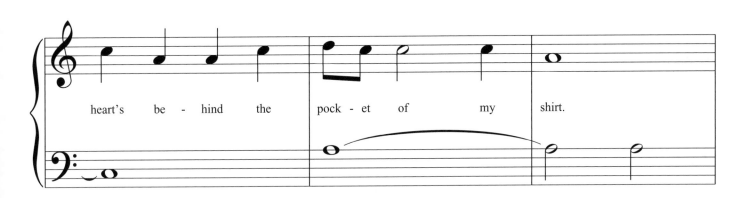

heart's be - hind the pock - et of my shirt.

I'll just keep roll - ing till I'm in the dirt, 'cause I'm a

trav - 'ller, oh, I'm a trav - 'ller.

I could - n't tell you, hon - ey, I don't know

where __ I'm go - ing, but I've got to go;

'cause ev - 'ry turn re - veals some oth - er road, and I'm a

trav - 'ller, oh, I'm a trav - 'ller.

To Coda ⊕

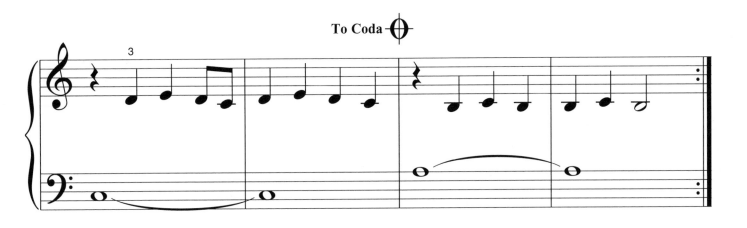

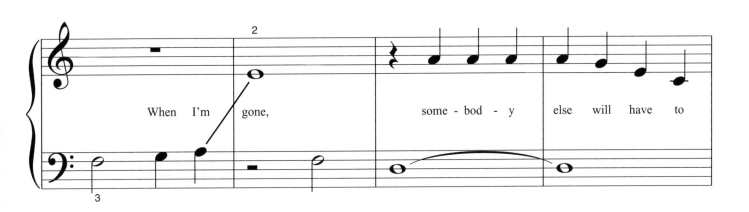

When I'm gone, some - bod - y else will have to

feel   this   wrong,   some - bod - y   else   will   have   to

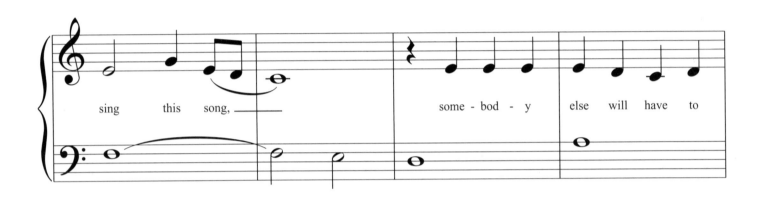

sing   this   song,   some - bod - y   else   will   have   to

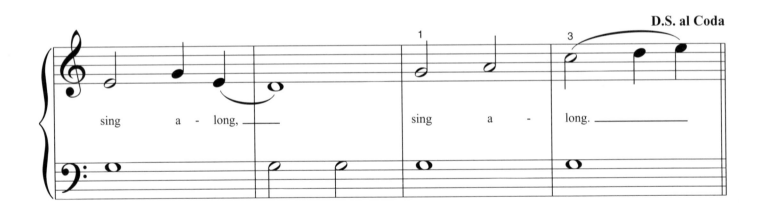

D.S. al Coda

sing   a - long,   sing   a -   long.

CODA

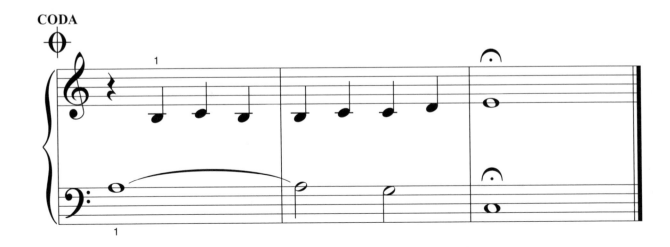

OPHELIA

Words and Music by JEREMY FRAITES
and WESLEY SCHULTZ

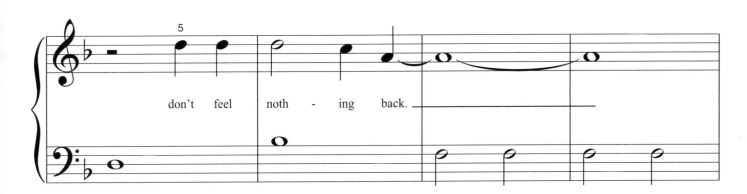

I, I've got a new girl - friend. She

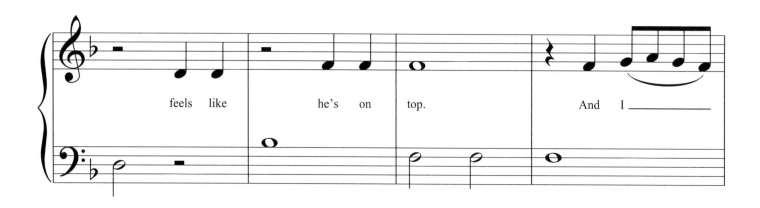

feels like he's on top. And I _____

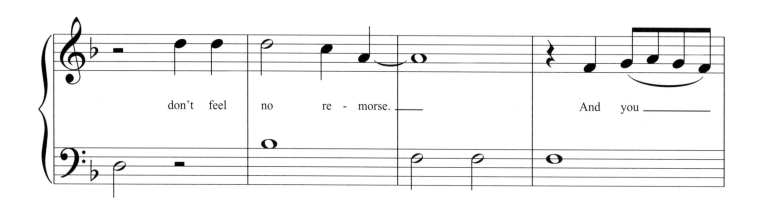

don't feel no re - morse. _____ And you _____

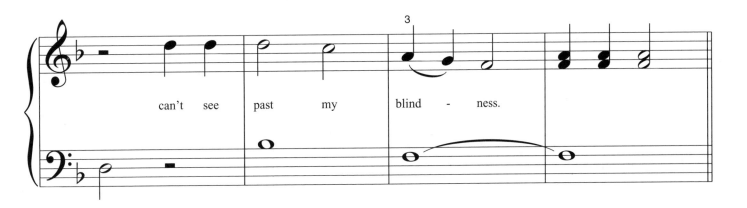

can't see past my blind - ness.

Oh, O - phe - li - a, _____ you've been on my mind, girl, since the flood. _____

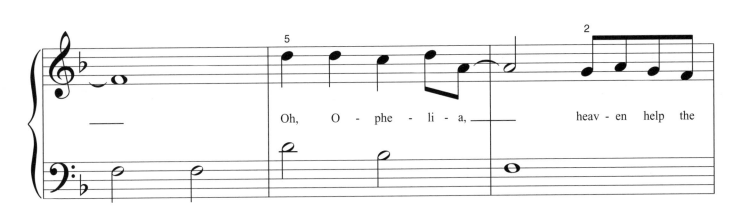

_____ Oh, O - phe - li - a, _____ heav - en help the

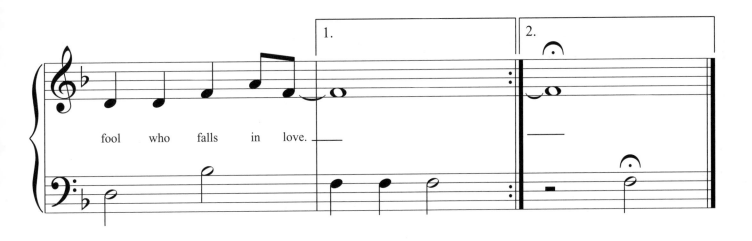

fool who falls in love. _____

1.

2.

7 YEARS

Words and Music by LUKAS FORCHHAMMER,
MORTEN RISTORP, STEFAN FORREST,
DAVID LABREL, CHRISTOPHER BROWN
and MORTEN PILEGAARD

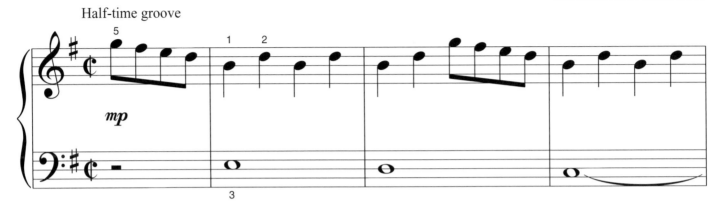

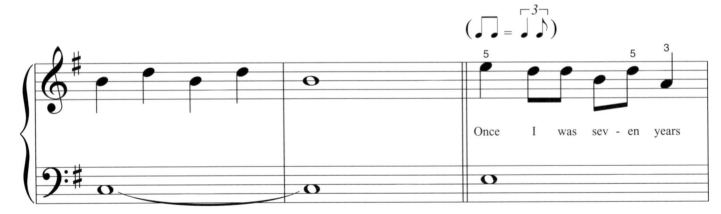

Once I was sev-en years

old, my ma-ma told me, "Go make your-self some friends or you'll be lone-ly." ___

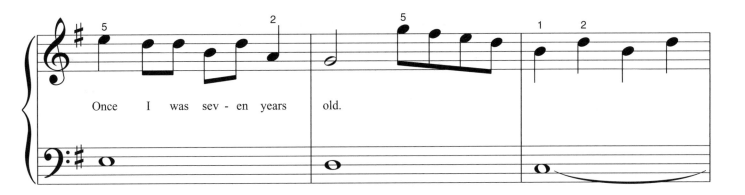

Once I was sev - en years old.

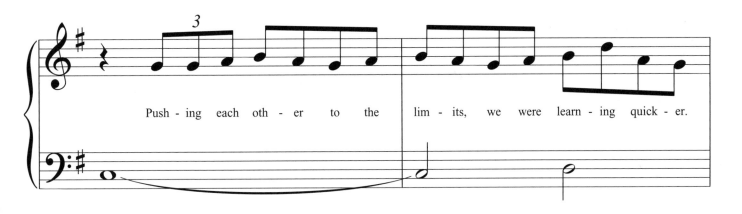

It was a big, big world, but we thought we were big - ger.

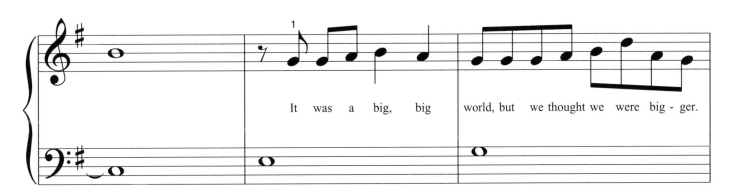

Push - ing each oth - er to the lim - its, we were learn - ing quick - er.

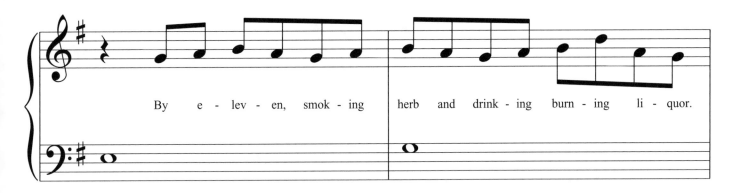

By e - lev - en, smok - ing herb and drink - ing burn - ing li - quor.

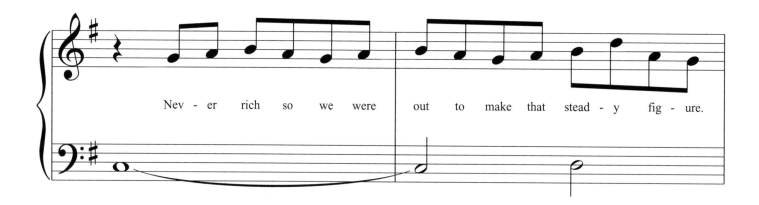

Nev - er rich so we were out to make that stead - y fig - ure.

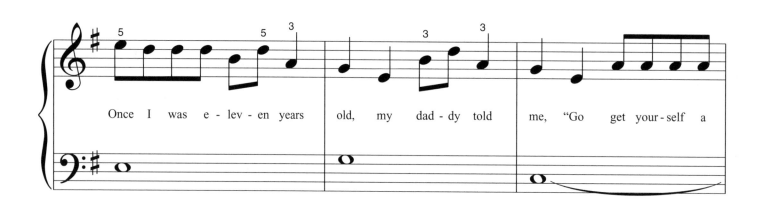

Once I was e - lev - en years old, my dad - dy told me, "Go get your - self a

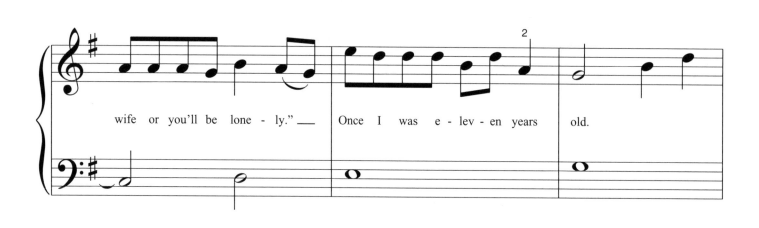

wife or you'll be lone - ly." __ Once I was e - lev - en years old.

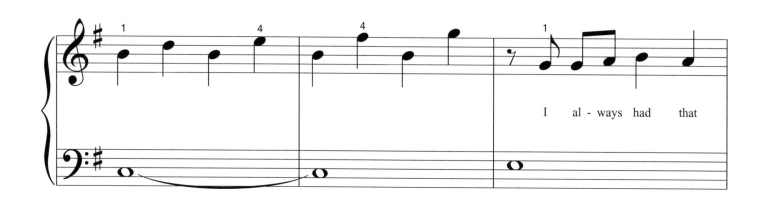

I al - ways had that

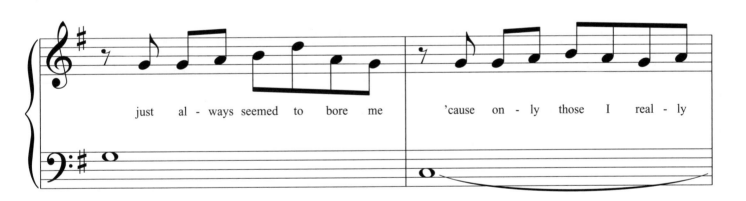

42

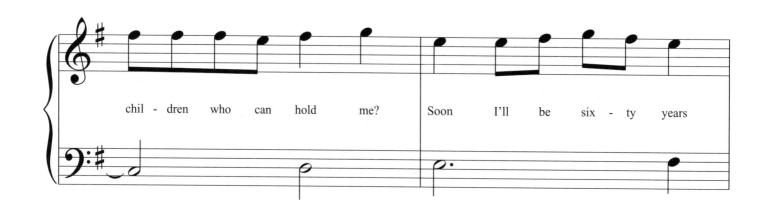

old.

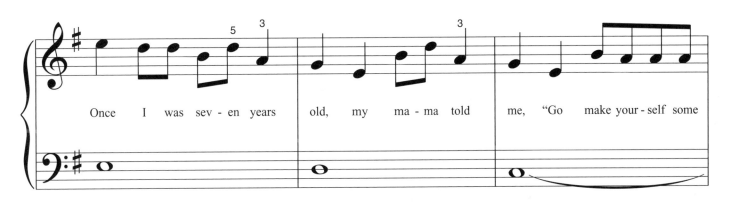

Once I was sev - en years old, my ma - ma told me, "Go make your - self some

friends or you'll be lone - ly." — Once I was sev - en years old.

Once I was sev - en years old.

WHEN WE WERE YOUNG

Words and Music by ADELE ADKINS
and TOBIAS JESSO JR.

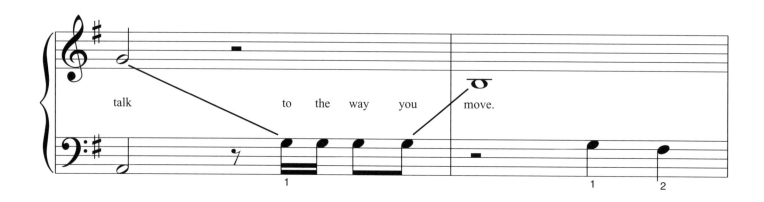

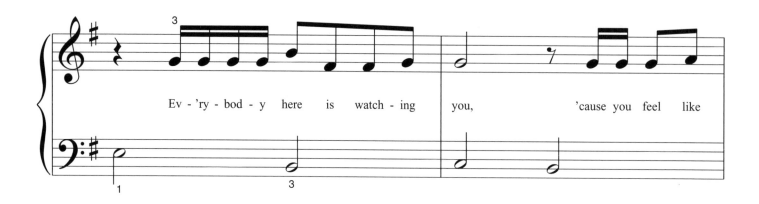

But if by chance you're here a - lone, can I have a

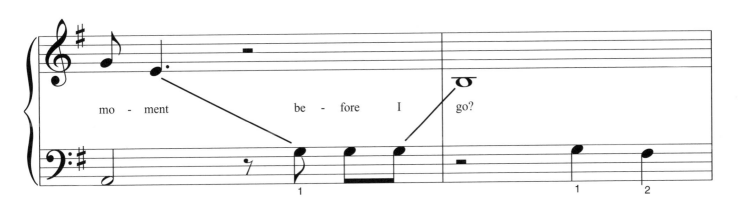

mo - ment be - fore I go?

'Cause I've been by my - self all night long, hop - ing you're

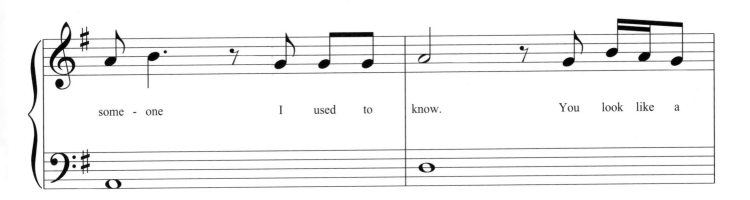

some - one I used to know. You look like a

mov - ie, you sound like a song; my God, this re -

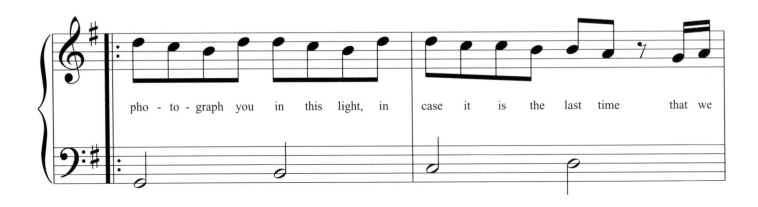

minds me of when we were young. Let me

pho - to - graph you in this light, in case it is the last time that we

might be ex - act - ly like we were be - fore we re - al - ized we were

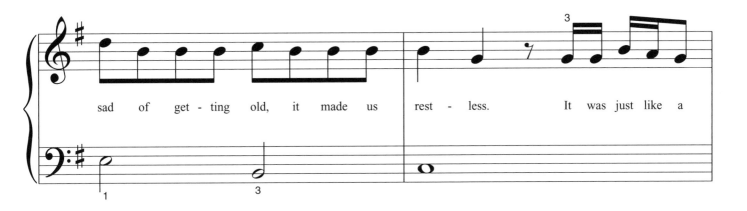

sad of get - ting old, it made us rest - less. It was just like a

mov - ie, it was just like a song. When

we were young, when we ___ were young, when we ___ were young, when we ___

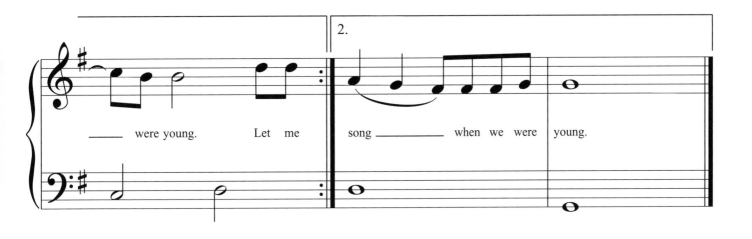

___ were young. Let me song ___ when we were young.